This Safari Book belongs to

... ...

To Vera, Noah, Emma and Jonah, my little global nomads. May you always carry the spirit of the African bush to every new home and may this song remain with you every Christmas.
All my love, WH

To Luka, my no longer so little bush-baby and Wolfgang, my father who taught me to love the bush. May there be many days and nights where we can marvel at the beauty of it all and hopefully pass that love on, so that the African bush remains with us and future generations.
MW

And to Yulia, the friend who made The Twelve Days of Christmas Safari a dream come true.
WH & MW

First published 2020 by Camerapix Publishers Ltd
www.camerapixmagazines.com
Text Copyright 2020 Wakanyi Hoffman
Illustrations Copyright 2020 Milena Weichelt
The right of Wakanyi Hoffman and Milena Weichelt to be identified as author and illustrator respectively has been asserted by them in accordance with the Copyright Act no. 12 of 2001 of The Republic of Kenya.

Third Edition 2021
Published by Springtime Books,
Great Britain.
All rights reserved.
ISBN: 978-1-8381746-9-9

Copyright Wakanyi Hoffman, 2021

All rights reserved. No part of this publication may be reproduced, stored in or introduced into a retrieval system or transmitted, in any form, or by any means (electronic, mechanical, photocopying, recording or otherwise) without the prior written permission from the publisher.

This book is sold subject to the condition that it shall not, by way of trade or otherwise, be lent, resold, hired out or otherwise circulated without the publisher's prior consent in any form of binding or cover other than in which it is published and without a similar condition including this condition being imposed on the subsequent purchaser.

Designed by Nazlı Tarcan
Illustrations by Milena Weichelt

THE TWELVE DAYS OF CHRISTMAS SAFARI

"If we do not do something to prevent it, Africa's animals, and the places in which they live, will be lost to our world, and her children, forever."

– Nelson Mandela, First President of the Republic of South Africa.

On the first day of Christmas
my tour guide said to me,
"There's a Starling in a fever tree."

On the second day of Christmas
my tour guide said to me,
"Two Dik-diks prancing
and a Starling in a fever tree."

On the third day of Christmas
my tour guide said to me,
"Three Leopards sleeping,
two Dik-diks prancing
and a Starling in a fever tree."

On the fourth day of Christmas
my tour guide said to me,
"Four Rhinos charging,
three Leopards sleeping,
two Dik-diks prancing
and a Starling in a fever tree."

On the fifth day of Christmas
my tour guide said to me,
"Five Lion Cubs!
Four Rhinos charging,
three Leopards sleeping,
two Dik-diks prancing
and a Starling in a fever tree."

On the sixth day of Christmas
my tour guide said to me,
"Six Hippos humming,
five Lion Cubs!
Four Rhinos charging,
three Leopards sleeping,
two Dik-diks prancing
and a Starling in a fever tree."

On the seventh day of Christmas
my tour guide said to me,
"Seven Zebras grazing,
six Hippos humming,
five Lion Cubs!
Four Rhinos charging,
three Leopards sleeping,
two Dik-diks prancing
and a Starling in a fever tree."

On the eighth day of Christmas
my tour guide said to me,
"Eight Giraffes are walking,
seven Zebras grazing,
six Hippos humming,
five Lion Cubs!
Four Rhinos charging,
three Leopards sleeping,
two Dik-diks prancing
and a Starling in a fever tree."

On the ninth day of Christmas
my tour guide said to me,
"Nine Buffaloes staring,
eight Giraffes are walking,
seven Zebras grazing,
six Hippos humming,
five Lion Cubs!
Four Rhinos charging,
three Leopards sleeping,
two Dik-diks prancing
and a Starling in a fever tree."

On the tenth day of Christmas
my tour guide said to me,
"Ten Flamingos flying,
nine Buffaloes staring,
eight Giraffes are walking,
seven Zebras grazing,
six Hippos humming,
five Lion Cubs!
Four Rhinos charging,
three Leopards sleeping,
two Dik-diks prancing
and a Starling in a fever tree."

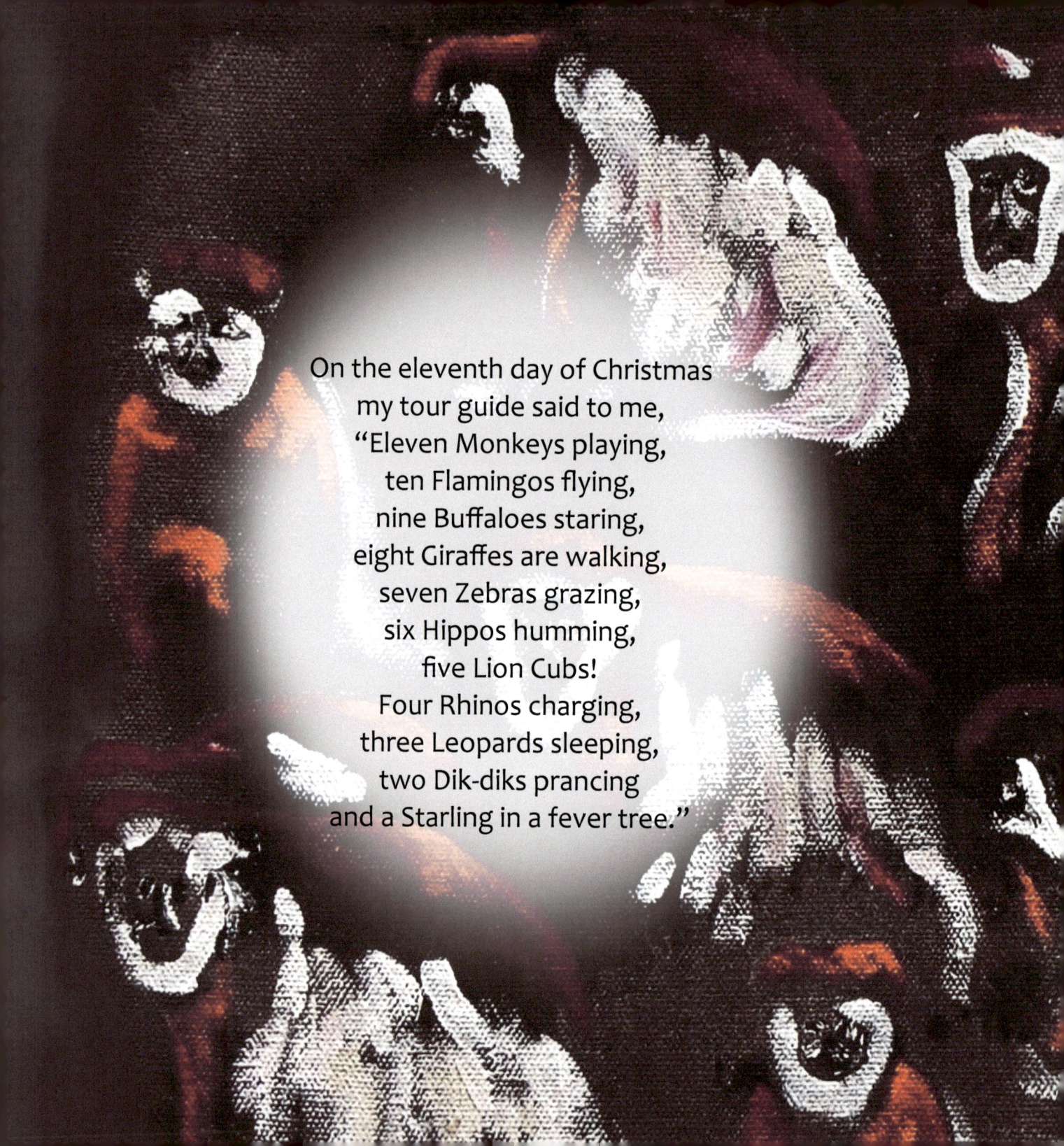

On the eleventh day of Christmas
my tour guide said to me,
"Eleven Monkeys playing,
ten Flamingos flying,
nine Buffaloes staring,
eight Giraffes are walking,
seven Zebras grazing,
six Hippos humming,
five Lion Cubs!
Four Rhinos charging,
three Leopards sleeping,
two Dik-diks prancing
and a Starling in a fever tree."

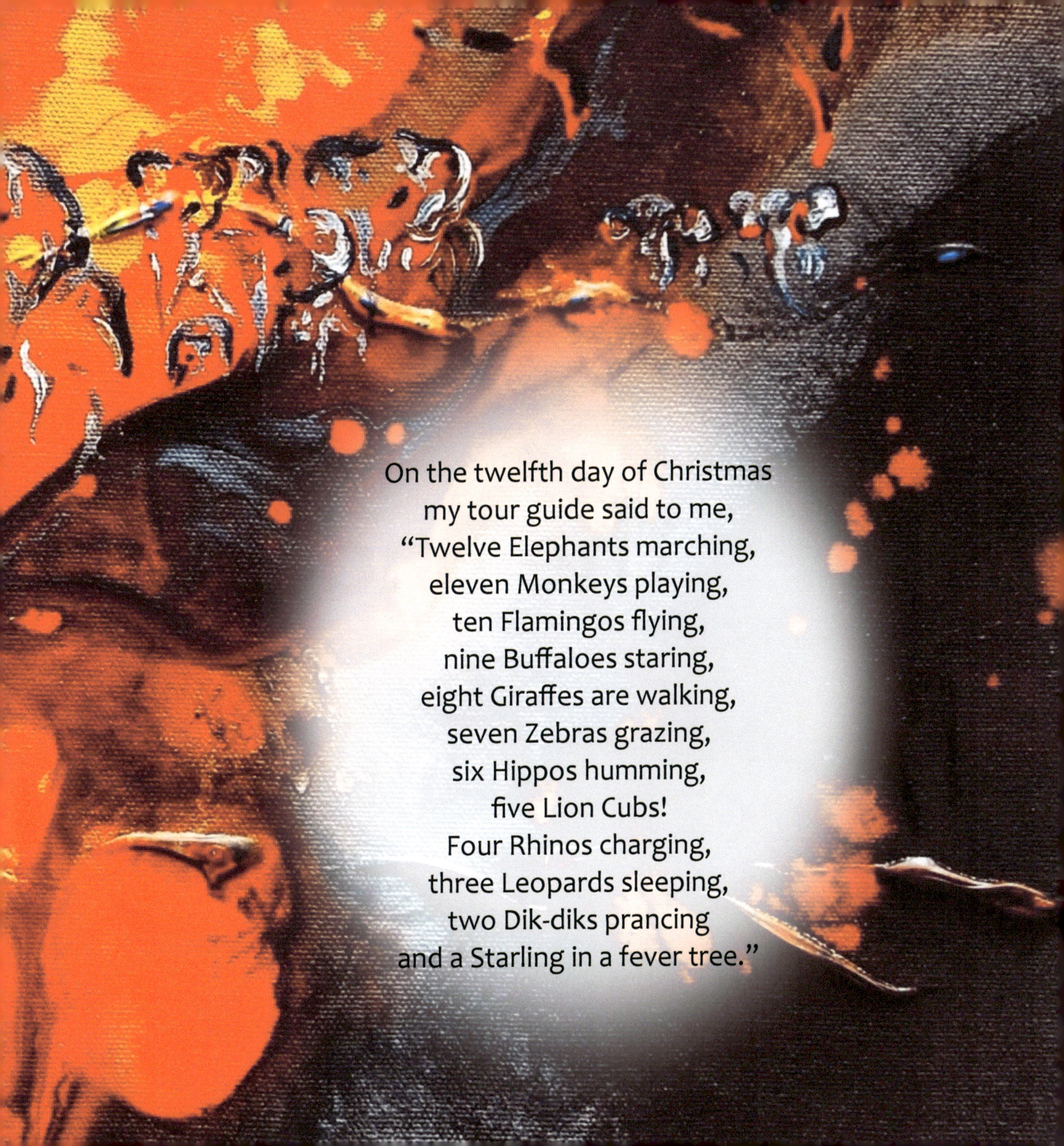

On the twelfth day of Christmas
my tour guide said to me,
"Twelve Elephants marching,
eleven Monkeys playing,
ten Flamingos flying,
nine Buffaloes staring,
eight Giraffes are walking,
seven Zebras grazing,
six Hippos humming,
five Lion Cubs!
Four Rhinos charging,
three Leopards sleeping,
two Dik-diks prancing
and a Starling in a fever tree."

The End

Safari packing list essentials:

Maasai Shuka
Picnic Basket
Drinking water in a reusable bottle
Sunhat
Sunglasses
Binoculars
Camera
Bird Book
Mammal Book
Note book
Walking shoes
Walking stick
Suncream
Adventure spirit
Patience
A sense of wonder maybe?

Wakanyi identifies as a world citizen, with strong Kenyan roots. Born in Nairobi, she grew up next to the world's only indigenous forest in a capital city. Much of her school days were spent running from monkeys that were keen to steal her lunch box! There was also, quite often, the odd warthog or two to escape from while trying to make it to class in time for the first bell. Surrounded by trees and with a clear view of the rolling Ngong Hills, telling nature stories became a habit from an early age. Wakanyi is passionate about preserving these stories and promoting the African indigenous way of oral storytelling. Together with her husband, they raise their four children around the world as global nomads, and 'The 12 days of Christmas Safari' began as a fun tradition to remind them of their African heritage. Wakanyi is currently based in the Netherlands, where she writes, edits, and performs folktales to a global audience. She also blogs about her family's travel tales on www.aglobalnomadshome.com and promotes African folktales through The African Folktales Project www.africanfolktalesproject.com

Milena was born in Hamburg and arrived in Africa when she was only one year old. She grew up in Kenya, where her father's love of safaris took her family to the bush frequently. Much to her parent's dismay, her main activity on those adventures was to collect all kinds of insects and take them along. She considered their car to be an "insect bush-taxi" and, in Milena's words, "You never leave friends behind." It was during those early years that Milena fell in love with nature and African wildlife. Milena's art is naturally inspired by her unforgettable childhood memories, and her pieces have found homes all around the world. As an active nature conservationist, Milena hopes to preserve and share her passion for a green environment by sharing art that speaks to children's hearts. She lives in Nairobi with her husband and son, and this is her first children's book illustration. For more information on her artwork, please visit www.milenasilverart.me

www.ingramcontent.com/pod-product-compliance
Ingram Content Group UK Ltd.
Pitfield, Milton Keynes, MK11 3LW, UK
UKHW060135240426
12048UKWH00002B/45